Quilting

Written by Biz Storms
Illustrated by June Bradford

KIDS CAN PRESS

To Alan, for always
To Turner, for the future — B.S.

Text © 2001 Biz Storms
Illustrations © 2001 June Bradford

KIDS CAN DO IT and the 🍁 logo are trademarks of Kids Can Press Ltd.

Kids Can Press acknowledges the financial support of the Government of Canada, through the BPIDP, for our publishing activity.

Published in Canada by
Kids Can Press Ltd.
29 Birch Avenue
Toronto, ON M4V 1E2

Published in the U.S. by
Kids Can Press Ltd.
2250 Military Road
Tonawanda, NY 14150

www.kidscanpress.com

Edited by Laurie Wark
Designed by Karen Powers
Photography by Frank Baldassarra
Printed in Hong Kong by Wing King Tong Company Limited

The hardcover edition of this book is smyth sewn casebound.
The paperback edition of this book is limp sewn with a drawn-on cover.

CM 01 0 9 8 7 6 5 4 3 2 1
CM PA 01 0 9 8 7 6 5 4 3 2 1

Canadian Cataloguing in Publication Data

Storms, Biz, 1955–
Quilting

(Kids can do it)
ISBN 1-55074-967-6 (bound)   ISBN 1-55074-805-X (pbk.)

1. Quilting — Juvenile literature. I. Bradford, June. II. Title. III. Series.
TT835.S747 2001   j746.46   C00-932967-6

Kids Can Press is a Nelvana company

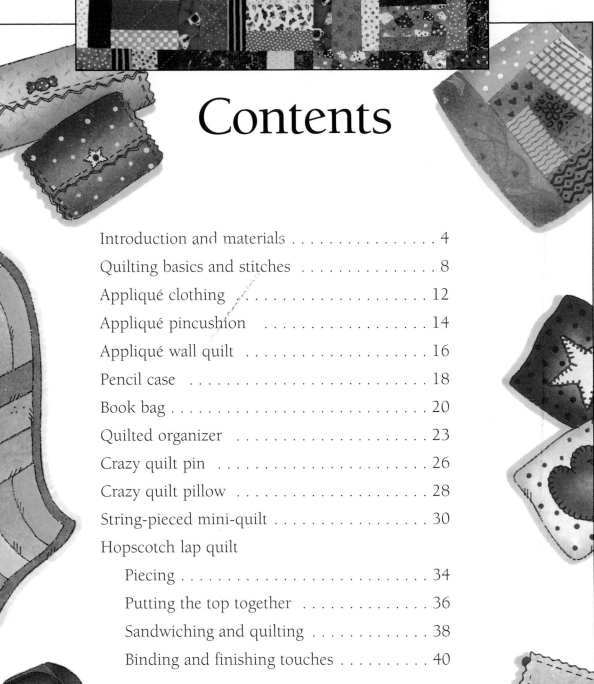

Contents

Introduction

The way you make a quilt today is the same way your great-great-great-great-grandmother made it 200 years ago. A quilt is layers of fabric and batting all stitched together. With this book you'll learn the basics of quilting and create some easy projects. Follow the crafts in order and you can build your quilting skills along the way. Start out small with a pincushion or pencil case and work your way up to a lap quilt.

Have a quilting party with friends. By sharing fabrics, you can create exciting color and pattern combinations. Try switching the quilting techniques with the different projects. Be as inventive as you like.
Happy quilting.

MATERIALS

Gather these basic sewing and quilting supplies and store them in a box. You may find some of these supplies at home, or at a quilt, craft or fabric shop.

Fabric

You can buy new fabric from a store or use leftover fabric you have around home. Old shirts, pajamas and dresses make good quilting fabric — 100% cotton works best. Wash new fabric to make sure the color doesn't run.

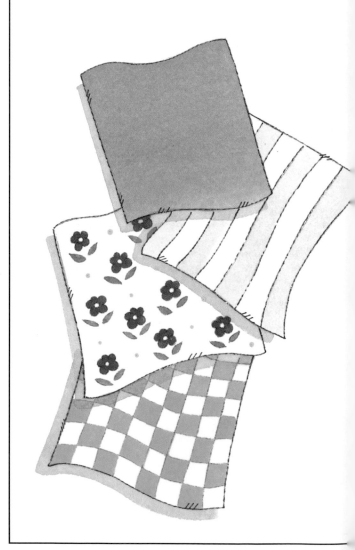

Thread and embroidery floss

Use 100% cotton thread or embroidery floss. When sewing with thread, pick a color that blends with your fabric. If you have several fabric colors, try beige or gray thread. If a project calls for embroidery floss, match it to your fabric or choose a contrasting color that really jumps out. Always separate the floss threads and use only two strands at a time. If you use more, the floss may knot or be too bulky.

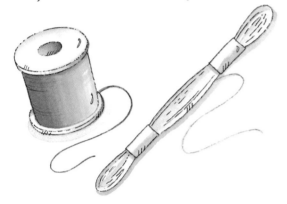

Needles

Try large needles, called sharps, for sewing with regular thread, and embroidery needles for embroidery floss. A large eye for easy threading and a sharp point for smooth sewing are important. You can wear a thimble to help push the needle through the fabric. An adhesive bandage works, as well.

Pins

Straight pins with plastic or colored heads are easy to hold and see. Make the pincushion on page 14 to hold your pins.

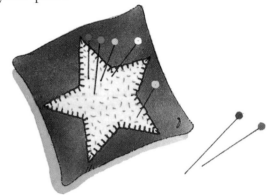

Scissors and pinking shears

You will need sharp scissors to cut fabric and thread. Pinking shears, with their zigzag edge, prevent fabric from fraying and make your projects look great.

Pencils and a ruler

To mark cutting and sewing lines, you will need a lead pencil for light-colored fabrics and a white or silver pencil for dark fabrics. Tailor's chalk and fabric pens can also be used. You'll need a see-through quilter's ruler with 0.5 cm (¼ in.) increments to mark seam allowances and cutting lines.

Quilt batting

Cotton batting is better than polyester because it is easy to cut and the edges don't fall apart. It comes in several sizes, so you can buy what you need. You may use cotton flannel instead, but your quilting will be flatter.

Iron

Always ask for an adult's help when using an iron. Use a regular iron on the cotton setting and press without steam.

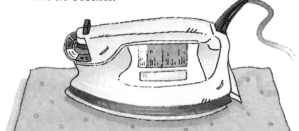

FUSIBLE WEB

Fusible web is a paper-backed adhesive used for appliqué projects. It works with the heat of an iron to attach two pieces of fabric. Pellon Wonder-Under, Steam-A-Seam or other brands are available. Read the label to make sure you can stitch through the web. Before following the instructions below, read the manufacturer's directions because some brands use slightly different methods.

1. With a pencil, trace or draw your appliqué shape onto the smooth, paper side of the fusible web.

2. Cut around the shape about 0.5 cm (¼ in.) outside the pencil line.

3. Place your shape, rough or glue side down, on the wrong side of the fabric.

4. Fuse the web to the fabric with an iron.

5. Use scissors to cut out the shape, along the pencil line.

6. Carefully peel off the paper backing.

7. Place your appliqué shape, glue side down, on the background fabric or piece of clothing and fuse with an iron.

8. Add a running stitch (see page 9) or a blanket stitch (see page 11) to secure the appliqué.

Quilting basics and stitches

As you quilt, refer to these pages whenever you need sewing information.

Fabric sides

Printed fabric has two sides — the right side, with the pattern, and the wrong side, where the pattern is missing or faded. Solid and woven fabrics are not printed, so either side can show.

Seam allowance

A seam allowance is the distance between the edge of the fabric and the stitching line. Quilters use a 0.5 cm (¼ in.) seam allowance. Before sewing fabric together, draw a light pencil line on the wrong side to stitch along. You won't see the line when the project is finished.

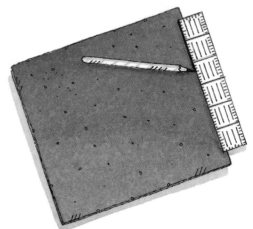

Threading and holding a needle

Cut about 45 cm (18 in.) of thread. Thread one end through the eye of the needle, leaving one end longer than the other. Hold the needle between your thumb and index finger. Use your middle finger to push the needle through the fabric.

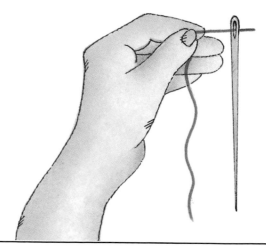

Loop knot

Begin and end your seams with this simple knot.

1. Make a small running stitch leaving a 2.5 cm (1 in.) tail.

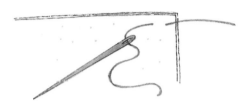

2. Backstitch (see page 10) over the first stitch but leave a tiny loop sticking up.

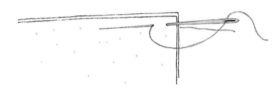

3. Slip the needle through the loop from the top and pull the loop closed.

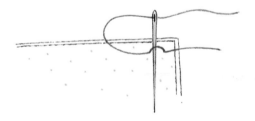

4. Make another backstitch and loop. Slip the needle up from the bottom and pull the loop closed. Trim the thread, leaving a 0.5 cm (¼ in.) tail.

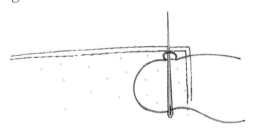

Running stitch

Use a small running stitch for seams and a medium running stitch for quilting or sandwiching.

1. Start at a corner with a loop knot. Push the needle down through both layers of fabric.

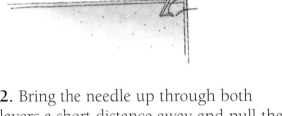

2. Bring the needle up through both layers a short distance away and pull the thread through. Repeat, making even stitches.

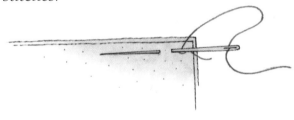

Changing thread

When you are running out of thread, make a loop knot and leave a 0.5 cm (¼ in.) tail. With a new piece of thread in the needle, make a loop knot close to the last one and continue sewing.

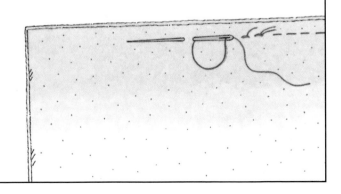

Backstitch

1. Make a small running stitch (see page 9).

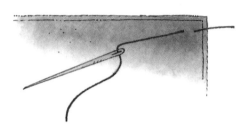

2. Make another stitch in the same spot with the needle going down and up through the same holes.

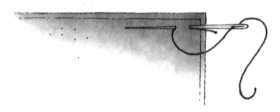

Blind stitch

This stitch is useful for closing a seam on a pincushion or pillow.

1. Lay the bottom piece of fabric over the top. Tuck the rough edges inside to form a folded edge, and pin in place.

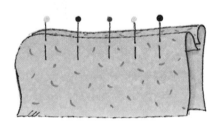

2. Make a small loop knot (see page 9) just to the right of the opening, as close to the seam as you can.

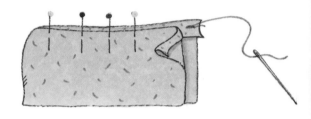

3. Start your stitch beside the loop knot and bring the needle up through the fold a short distance away.

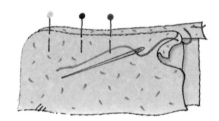

4. Repeat with small, even stitches close to the folded edge, until the opening is closed. Finish with a backstitch and a loop knot.

Blanket stitch

1. With two strands of knotted embroidery floss in your needle, bring the needle up from the back of the fabric just outside the edge of the appliqué. Pull the floss through until the knot stops it.

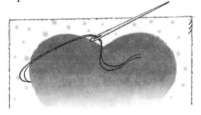

2. Hold the floss to the side of the appliqué with your thumb.

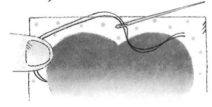

3. Insert the needle up and in about 0.5 cm (¼ in.). Bring the tip of the needle out at the edge of the appliqué. Pull the needle above the floss held by your thumb.

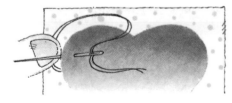

4. Release the floss and pull gently on the needle until the floss lies flat on the edge of the appliqué.

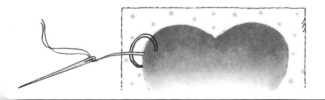

5. Repeat steps 2 to 4 as you stitch away from yourself. Finish by pulling the floss to the back and tying a loop knot (see page 9).

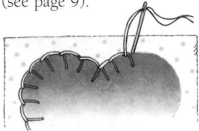

Sewing a seam

These are the basic steps in sewing a seam. The instructions for each project tell you which stitch to use and when.

1. Put two pieces of fabric right sides together and pin.

2. Make a loop knot (see page 9) at the right-hand side (at the left-hand side if you are left-handed).

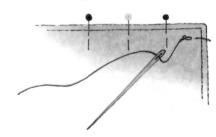

3. Using a small running stitch (see page 9), sew to the other side.

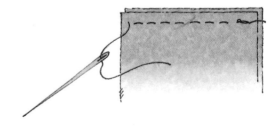

4. Make a loop knot (see page 9). Cut the thread.

Appliqué clothing

Learn how to fuse and blanket stitch appliqué shapes. Go wild with colors and shapes — you can even add your name.

YOU WILL NEED

- clothing (clean and pressed)
- fabric scraps
- fusible web
- embroidery floss
- cookie cutters or shapes to trace
- scissors, embroidery needles, iron, pencil

1 Draw shapes using the cookie cutters or trace the shapes on the next page onto the smooth, paper side of the fusible web. Cut around them about 0.5 cm (1/4 in.) outside the pencil line.

2 Fuse the shapes to the wrong side of the fabric scraps (see page 6).

3 Cut out the shapes using the pencil line as your guide. Peel off the paper backing.

4 Fuse the appliqué shapes to the clothing (see page 6).

5 Blanket stitch (see page 11) around the appliqués.

OTHER IDEAS

To add a name, draw fat letters on scrap paper, cut them out, and turn them over before tracing onto the fusible web. Otherwise, the appliqué letters will be backwards.

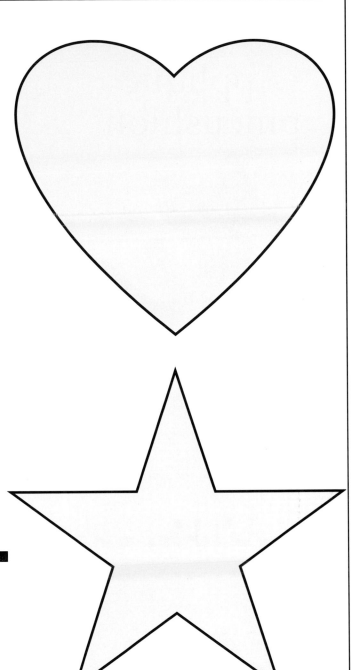

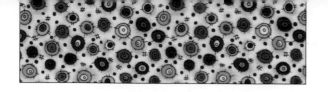

Appliqué pincushion

Create a distinct and useful gift for anyone who sews or quilts.

YOU WILL NEED

- a 13 cm x 13 cm (5 in. x 5 in.) fabric square for the top
- a 13 cm x 13 cm (5 in. x 5 in.) fabric square for the back
- a fabric scrap
- fusible web
- embroidery floss
- cotton or polyester stuffing
- scissors, thread, sewing and embroidery needles, pins, iron, pencil, ruler

1 Trace a shape from page 13 onto the smooth, paper side of the fusible web. Cut around it about 0.5 cm (¼ in.) outside the pencil line.

2 Fuse the shape to the wrong side of the fabric scrap (see page 6).

3 Cut out the shape using the pencil line as your guide. Peel off the paper backing.

4 Fuse the shape to the right side of the quilt top square (see page 6). Blanket stitch with floss around the shape (see page 11).

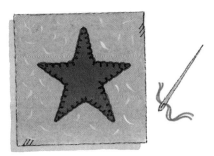

5 Place the quilt back square wrong side up. Lightly mark a 0.5 cm (¹/₄ in.) seam allowance along all sides with a pencil.

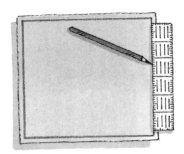

6 Pin the squares right sides together. Use a small running stitch with thread (see page 9) along the pencil line, leaving a 7.5 cm (3 in.) opening on one side. Backstitch (see page 10) several times at each side of the opening. Remove the pins as you sew.

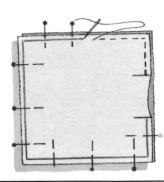

7 Turn the square right side out. Fill with stuffing until it's almost firm.

8 Pin the opening shut and blind stitch (see page 10). Start and stop with a loop knot (see page 9). Remove the pins.

OTHER IDEAS

• Make smaller squares and fill with lavender or potpourri for a sachet.

• Sew on a few buttons or beads before step 5, leaving the seam allowance clear.

Appliqué wall quilt

Paint a picture with fabric and thread.

YOU WILL NEED

- a 40 cm x 50 cm (16 in. x 20 in.) piece of fabric for the quilt top
- a 40 cm x 50 cm (16 in. x 20 in.) piece of fabric for the quilt back
- fabric scraps • fusible web
- embroidery floss and needle
- a 40 cm x 50 cm (16 in. x 20 in.) piece of cotton batting
- scissors, pinking shears, pins, iron, pencil, ruler

1 Trace or draw flower and leaf shapes (or any shapes you like) onto the smooth, paper side of the fusible web. Cut around them about 0.5 cm (¼ in.) outside the pencil line.

2 Fuse the shapes to the wrong side of the fabric scraps (see page 6). Cut out the shapes using the pencil line as a guide. Peel off the paper backing.

3 Fuse the shapes to the right side of the quilt top fabric (see page 6). Blanket stitch around the shapes (see page 11).

4 To sandwich your quilt, place the quilt back fabric right side down and put the batting on it. Lay the quilt top right side up on the batting. Keeping the edges lined up, pin the quilt sandwich together.

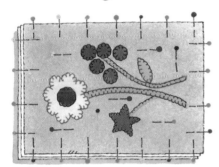

5 With two strands of embroidery floss, use a medium running stitch (see page 9) to sew 2 cm (³/4 in.) inside the edges. Start and stop with a loop knot (see page 9). Remove the pins as you sew.

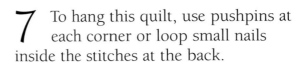

6 Carefully cut along the edges with pinking shears.

7 To hang this quilt, use pushpins at each corner or loop small nails inside the stitches at the back.

OTHER IDEAS

For a more decorative look, use a dowel to hang your quilt. When completing step 5, leave an opening in the stitching on opposite sides, the same distance from the top. Slide the dowel between the backing and the batting so the ends stick out. Hang from small nails or tie a ribbon at each end of the dowel and hang from a nail.

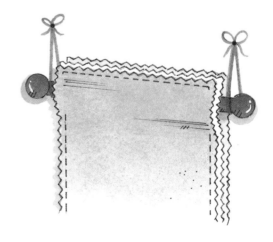

Pencil case

Make this easy project in an afternoon. Try using different fabrics for the inside and outside.

YOU WILL NEED

- a 25 cm x 25 cm (10 in. x 10 in.) square of fabric for the outside
- a 25 cm x 25 cm (10 in. x 10 in.) square of fabric for the inside
- a 25 cm x 25 cm (10 in. x 10 in.) square of cotton batting
- embroidery floss
- a snap closure or Velcro
- a button, bead or tassel (optional)
- scissors, pinking shears, embroidery needles, pins, pencil, ruler

1 Draw a light pencil line 2 cm (3/4 in.) in from all edges on the right side of the outside fabric.

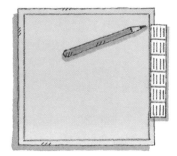

2 To sandwich the layers, place the inside fabric right side down and put the batting on it. Lay the outside fabric right side up on the batting. Keeping the edges lined up, pin the quilt sandwich together.

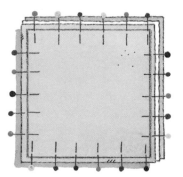

3 With two strands of embroidery floss, use a medium running stitch (see page 9) to sew along the pencil line. Start and stop with a loop knot (see page 9). Remove the pins as you sew.

4 Carefully cut along the edges with pinking shears.

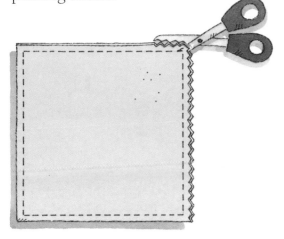

5 Turn the quilt sandwich over so the inside fabric is right side up. Fold one end over 8 cm (3½ in.) and pin. With two strands of embroidery floss, use a medium running stitch (see page 9) to sew the fold from bottom to top along the existing stitching. Start with several backstitches (see page 10) and end with a loop knot (see page 9). Remove the pins as you sew.

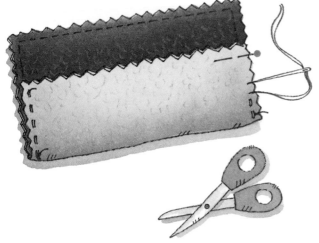

6 Fold the other end over to close the opening. With a pencil, mark where you want the snap or Velcro closure. Stitch it on securely with embroidery floss.

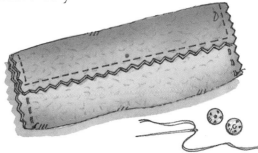

7 Stitch a button, bead or tassel on the flap just above the snap or Velcro.

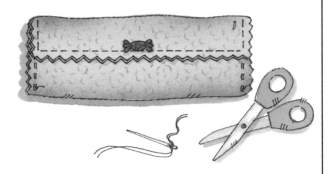

OTHER IDEAS

- Change the size or shape of the fabric to make a change purse or a pouch for secret treasures.

- Make a purse by stitching a length of ribbon on the fold line before you complete step 6.

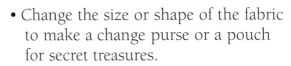

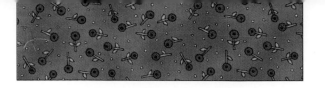

Book bag

Have fun with your choice of fabric for this easy project. It makes a nice present.

YOU WILL NEED

- a 40 cm x 75 cm (16 in. x 30 in.) piece of fabric for the outside
- a 40 cm x 75 cm (16 in. x 30 in.) piece of fabric for the inside
- two 20 cm x 60 cm (8 in. x 24 in.) pieces of fabric for the straps
- a 35 cm x 70 cm (14 in. x 28 in.) piece of cotton batting
- embroidery floss
- scissors, thread, sewing and embroidery needles, pins, ruler

1 Lay one of the strap pieces right side down. Fold the lengthwise edges in to meet in the middle.

2 Fold this strip in half and pin. It will now measure 5 cm x 60 cm (2 in. x 24 in.).

3 Sew along the lengthwise opening with a small running stitch (see page 9). Remove the pins as you sew. Repeat steps 1 to 3 with the other strap piece.

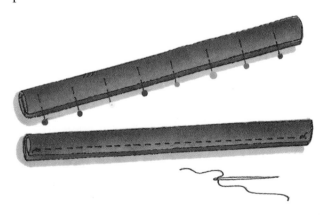

4 Lay the piece of outside fabric right side down. Put the batting on top. Leave an even margin on all sides.

5 Fold the bottom fabric over the edge of the batting on all sides and pin.

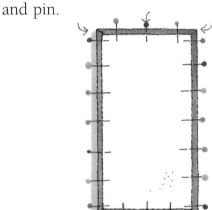

6 Lay the piece of inside fabric right side up on the batting. Leave an even overhang on all sides.

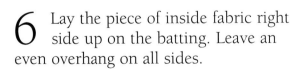

7 Tuck this overhang inside so all the folded edges line up. Pin the three layers together to form a quilt sandwich.

8 Insert the ends of the straps 7.5 cm (3 in.) in from each corner, on the 35 cm (14 in.) sides, and pin. Hold your book bag by the straps to make sure that they are the same length and haven't become twisted. Make any adjustments needed.

Instructions continue on the next page ☞

9 With two strands of embroidery floss, use a medium running stitch (see page 9) to sew 1.5 cm (½ in.) in from the edge, around all sides. Backstitch (see page 10) several times when sewing across the straps and at each corner. Start and stop with a loop knot (see page 9). Remove the pins as you sew.

10 With the inside fabric on top, fold the sandwich in half and pin. It should measure approximately 35 cm x 35 cm (14 in. x 14 in.). With two strands of embroidery floss, use a medium running stitch (see page 9) to sew both sides together from bottom to top, along the existing stitching. Start and stop with a loop knot (see page 9). Remove the pins as you sew.

OTHER IDEAS

- Change the fabric size to make the bag larger or smaller.

- Add appliqué designs to the sides before you sandwich the layers together.

- Crazy quilt (see page 26) or string-piece (see page 30) the outside fabric.

- Sew on decorations such as buttons, beads or small ornaments after step 10.

Quilted organizer

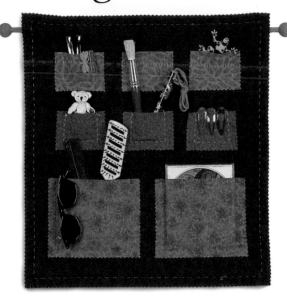

Get organized with this handy holder.

1 Draw a faint pencil line 2 cm (³/₄ in.) in from all edges on the right side of the quilt top fabric.

2 Sandwich the fabric layers together. Place the quilt back fabric right side down and put the batting on it. Lay the quilt top fabric on top of the batting, right side up. Keeping the edges lined up, pin the quilt sandwich together.

Instructions continue on the next page ☞

3 With two strands of embroidery floss, use a medium running stitch (see page 9) to sew along the pencil line. Start and stop with a loop knot (see page 9). Remove the pins as you sew.

4 Fold your pocket fabrics in half so that you have six 10 cm x 7.5 cm (4 in. x 3 in.) pockets and two 18 cm x 15 cm (7 in. x 6 in.) pockets. Press the folds with an iron.

5 Draw a faint pencil line on the three open sides of each pocket 2 cm (³/4 in.) in from the edge.

6 With pinking shears, carefully cut a new edge on all sides of the quilt sandwich and on the three open sides of the pockets.

7 Following the diagram below, pin the pockets to the quilt sandwich with the folds toward the top. With two strands of embroidery floss, use a medium running stitch (see page 9) to sew along the pencil lines. Start and stop with a loop knot (see page 9). Remove the pins as you sew.

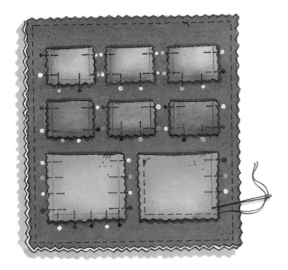

8 To hang this organizer, use pushpins or thumbtacks across the top or loop small nails inside the stitches at the back.

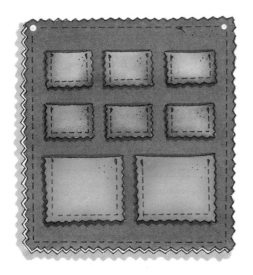

OTHER IDEAS

• For a more decorative look, hang the organizer from a dowel (see page 17).

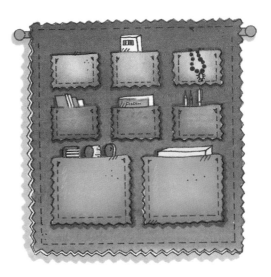

• Add a secret pocket to the back to hide special things.

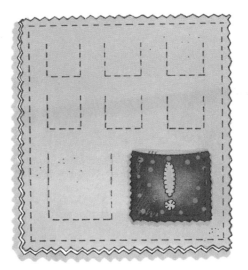

Crazy quilt pin

Use cookie cutters or draw any shape you like to make a pin or barrette.

YOU WILL NEED

- fabric scraps
- cotton batting
- a pin closure or barrette clip
- embroidery floss
- beads, buttons or charms (optional)
- scissors, pinking shears, thread, sewing and embroidery needles, pins, iron, pencil, ruler

1 Cut a 10 cm x 10 cm (4 in. x 4 in.) square from the batting and from a fabric scrap.

2 Pin a fabric scrap, right side up, to the batting. Pin another scrap on top of the first scrap, right side down. With thread, use a small running stitch (see page 9) to sew along one edge. Start and stop with a loop knot (see page 9). Remove the pins as you sew.

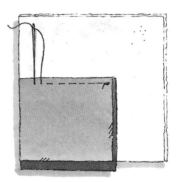

3 Flip open the top fabric and press flat with your fingers.

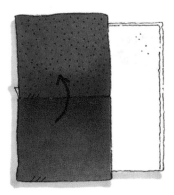

4 Pin another scrap right side down, lining up one edge. Sew, remove pins, flip open, and press flat with your fingers. Repeat this step until the batting is completely covered. Press with an iron.

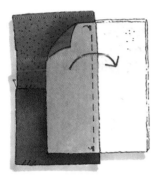

5 With a pencil, lightly trace a shape onto the crazy quilted piece for your cutting line. Trace a second line 0.5 cm (¼ in.) inside the first line for your sewing line.

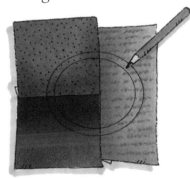

6 Sew on beads, buttons or charms if you like, but not too close to the pencil lines.

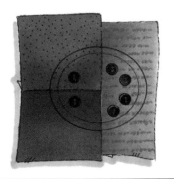

7 Pin the quilted piece to the wrong side of the backing fabric. With two strands of embroidery floss, use a medium running stitch (see page 9) to sew along the inside pencil line. Start and stop with a loop knot (see page 9). Remove the pins as you sew.

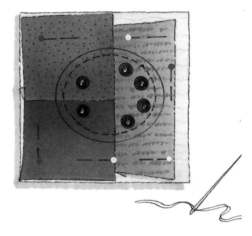

8 Carefully trim along the outside pencil line with pinking shears. With thread, sew the pin closure or barrette clip onto the back.

Crazy quilt pillow

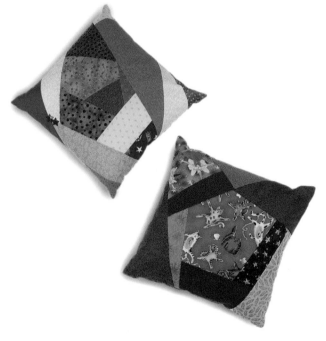

Have fun playing with fabric for this pillow.
It will look great in your room.

YOU WILL NEED

- fabric scraps
- a 40 cm x 40 cm (16 in. x 16 in.) piece of fabric scrap
- a 40 cm x 40 cm (16 in. x 16 in.) piece of fabric for the backing
- a 35 cm (14 in.) pillow form (available at craft or sewing supply shops)
- scissors, thread, sewing needles, pins, iron, pencil, ruler

1 Pin a fabric scrap, right side up, to the 40 cm x 40 cm (16 in. x 16 in.) piece of fabric scrap. Pin another scrap, on top of the first scrap, right side down.

2 Sew along one edge with a small running stitch (see page 9). Start and stop with a loop knot (see page 9). Remove the pins, flip open the top fabric, and press flat with your fingers.

3 Pin another scrap right side down, lining up one edge. Sew, remove pins, flip open, and press flat with your fingers.

4 Repeat step 3 until the 40 cm x 40 cm (16 in. x 16 in.) fabric scrap is covered. Press with an iron.

5 Turn the crazy quilted piece over and trim off the extra fabric.

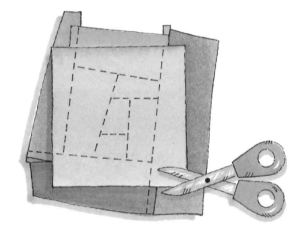

6 Place the backing fabric wrong side up. Lightly mark a 2 cm (3/4 in.) seam allowance along all sides with a pencil. Mark a 20 cm (8 in.) opening on one side.

7 Pin the crazy quilted piece and the backing fabric right sides together. Stitch along the pencil line around all sides, leaving the opening on one side. Use a small running stitch (see page 9) and backstitch several times (see page 10) at each side of the opening. Remove the pins as you sew.

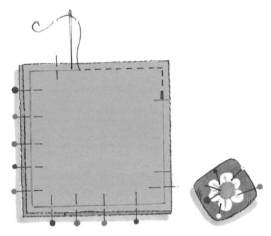

8 Turn the square right side out and push the pillow form inside. Pin the opening shut and blind stitch (see page 10). Start and stop with a loop knot (see page 9). Remove the pins.

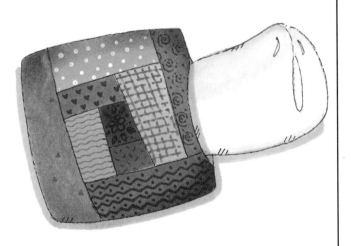

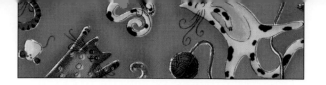

String-pieced mini-quilt

Learn one of the oldest methods of quilt making, called string-piecing. Your finished quilt could be used as a table quilt.

YOU WILL NEED

- seven strips of fabric, each approximately 33 cm x 7.5 cm (13 in. x 3 in.)
- a 33 cm x 40 cm (13 in. x 16 in.) piece of cotton batting
- a 38 cm x 45 cm (15 in. x 18 in.) piece of fabric for the backing
- embroidery floss
- scissors, thread, sewing and embroidery needles, pins, iron, pencil, ruler

1 Pin a strip of fabric, right side up, across the middle of the batting. Pin another strip, on top of the first strip, right side down. Lightly mark a 0.5 cm (¼ in.) seam allowance along one edge with a pencil.

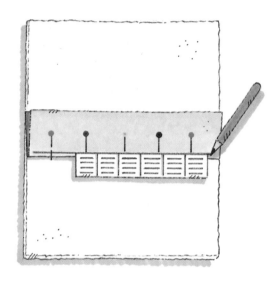

2 Sew along the pencil line with a small running stitch (see page 9). Start and stop with a loop knot (see page 9).

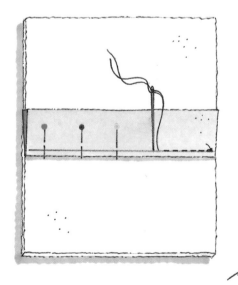

3 Remove the pins as you sew. Flip open the top strip, and press flat with your fingers.

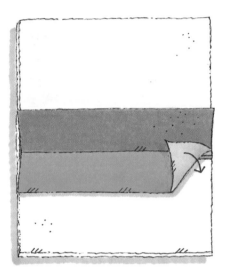

5 Repeat step 4 until the batting is covered. Press with an iron.

4 Pin another strip, right side down, along one edge. Mark the seam allowance and stitch. Remove the pins, flip open the top strip, and press flat with your fingers.

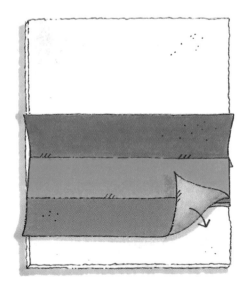

6 Turn the quilt top over and trim off the ends of the strips.

Instructions continue on the next page ☞

7 To sandwich the quilt, put the backing fabric right side down. Lay the quilt top in the middle of the backing fabric, right side up, with an even margin of backing fabric on all sides. Pin the quilt sandwich together.

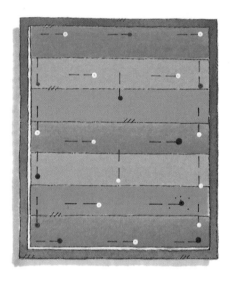

9 With two strands of embroidery floss, use a medium running stitch (see page 9) to sew along the pencil lines. Start and stop with a loop knot (see page 9) at the edges of the quilt top. Remove the pins.

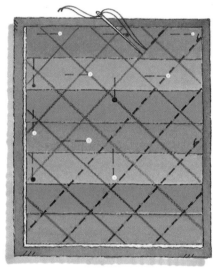

8 Follow the diagram to draw seven or eight faint pencil lines diagonally across the quilt top.

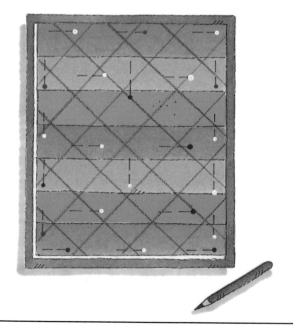

10 Fold the 45 cm (18 in.) edges of the backing fabric in half toward the quilt top. Fold again over the top of the quilt to cover the raw edges and the quilting knots. Pin in place. Fold the 38 cm (15 in.) edges the same way and pin in place.

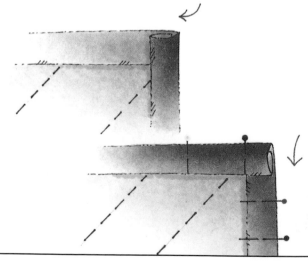

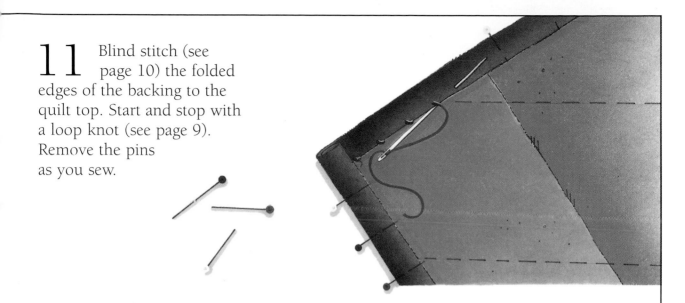

11 Blind stitch (see page 10) the folded edges of the backing to the quilt top. Start and stop with a loop knot (see page 9). Remove the pins as you sew.

OTHER IDEAS

• Personalize your quilt by adding appliqué shapes or your initials.

• Use fabric with a color or pattern theme to make holiday or seasonal quilts.

• Make the quilt larger for a stuffed animal to snuggle under.

• Make a memory quilt using fabric from your old clothes.

• Try writing messages with permanent pens, or draw designs on plain fabrics.

Hopscotch lap quilt

This is a larger project than the others and will take more time to complete. Find a place where you can leave your quilting set up. Experiment with the width and alignment of the strips.

PIECING

1 Lightly mark a 0.5 cm (¼ in.) seam allowance along all sides of a square with a pencil.

2 Place the square unmarked side up. Pin a strip of fabric, right side up, across the middle of the square. Pin another strip on top of the first strip right side down. Lightly mark a 0.5 cm (¼ in.) seam allowance along one edge with a pencil.

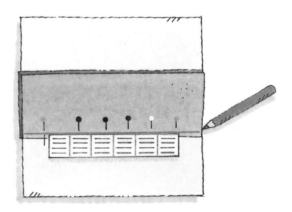

3 Sew along the pencil line with a small running stitch (see page 9). Start and stop with a loop knot (see page 9). Remove the pins as you sew. Flip open the top strip, and press flat with your fingers.

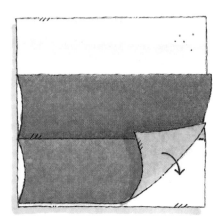

4 Pin another strip, right side down, along one edge. Mark the seam allowance and stitch. Remove the pins, flip open the top strip, and press flat with your fingers.

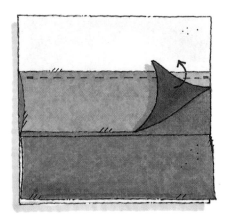

5 Repeat step 4 until the square is covered. Press with an iron.

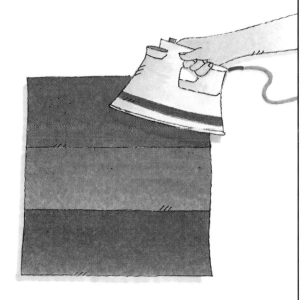

6 Turn the square over and trim off the ends of the strips.

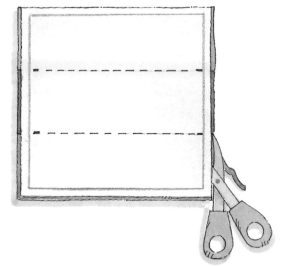

7 Repeat steps 1 to 6 for the remaining 34 squares.

Instructions continue on the next page ☞

PUTTING THE TOP TOGETHER

1 Lay the squares on a table or bed in a rectangle measuring five squares by seven squares. Move the squares around until you like the way they look. The direction of the strips should be the same as shown below.

2 Separate the squares into seven rows of five.

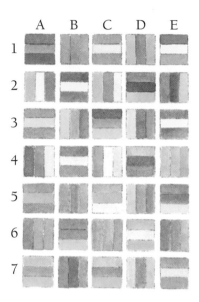

3 Starting with row 1, pin squares **A** and **B**, right sides together, along the edge where they touch. Sew along the pencil line using a small running stitch (see page 9). Start and stop with a loop knot (see page 9). Remove the pins as you sew.

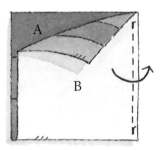

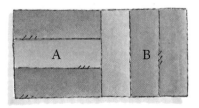

4 Press the seam open with an iron and put the stitched squares back where they came from. Make sure the design is still correct. Sew square **C** to the side of square **B**, as shown.

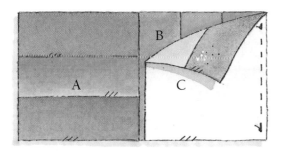

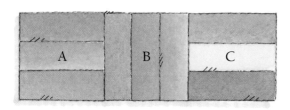

5 Finish the row by stitching on squares **D** and **E**.

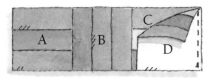

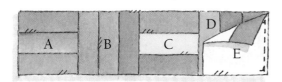

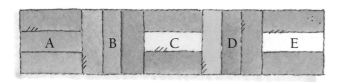

6 Sew the remaining six rows together, following steps 3 to 5.

7 Pin rows 1 and 2, right sides together. Make sure the seam lines go together. Sew along the pencil lines using a small running stitch (see page 9), and backstitch (see page 10) several times when you stitch across a seam line. Start and stop with a loop knot (see page 9). Remove the pins as you sew.

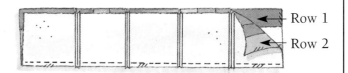

8 Press the seam open with an iron and put the stitched rows back where they came from. Make sure the design is still correct. Sew row 3 to row 2, as shown.

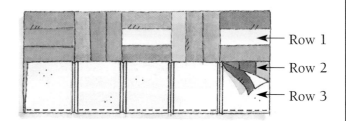

9 Sew the remaining rows together, following steps 7 and 8.

Instructions continue on the next page ☞

SANDWICHING AND QUILTING

1 Smooth out the batting and place your quilt top on it. Pin them together and cut the batting to the same size as the quilt top. Remove the pins.

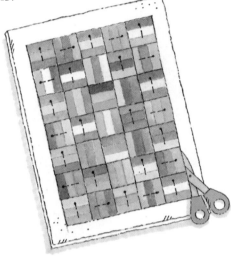

2 Iron the quilt backing to remove all wrinkles. Lay the quilt top on the backing and pin together. Cut the back so that it is 5 cm (2 in.) wider than the quilt top on all four sides. Remove the pins.

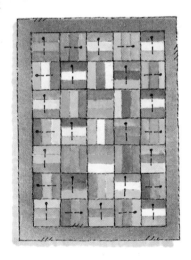

3 To sandwich the quilt, lay the quilt backing, right side down, on the floor or a large table. Tape down the corners and sides with masking tape to prevent it from moving.

4 Place the batting in the middle of the backing. Leave an even margin on all sides. Lay the quilt top on the batting, right side up. Keep the edges lined up so you can still see the backing fabric on all sides.

5 Pin the quilt sandwich together with safety pins. Space the pins about 10 cm (4 in.) apart.

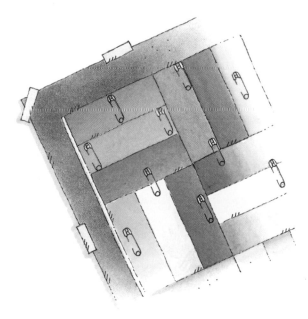

6 Draw a pencil **X** from corner to corner on each square. These **X**'s form a large grid pattern. Remove the tape and pick the quilt sandwich off the floor or table.

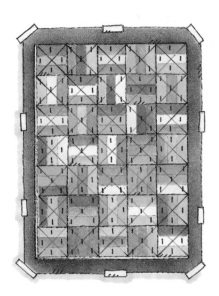

7 With two strands of embroidery floss, use a medium running stitch (see page 9) to sew along the pencil lines. Start on one side of the quilt top and work your way across to the other side. Start and stop with a loop knot (see page 9). Remove only the safety pins that get in your way as you stitch.

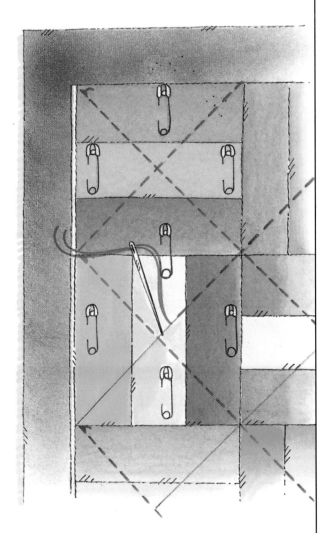

8 When you have stitched along every line, remove the remaining safety pins.

Instructions continue on the next page ☞

BINDING

1 Fold the long edges of the backing fabric in half toward the quilt top. Fold again over the top of the quilt to cover the raw edges. Pin in place.

2 Fold the short edges the same way and pin in place.

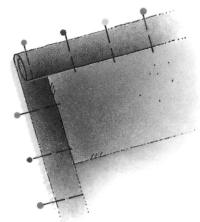

3 Blind stitch (see page 10) the folded edges of the backing to the quilt top. Start and stop with a loop knot (see page 9). Remove the pins as you sew.

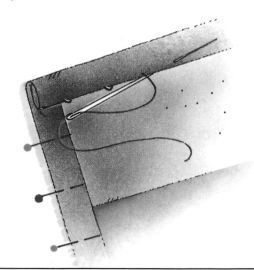

FINISHING TOUCHES

Just as an artist signs a piece of artwork, you should sew a label onto your quilt. Using a pen with permanent ink, print your information on a 20 cm (4 in.) square of plain fabric. Include your name, the date, the place and the name of the person you made it for if it's a gift. You can also add a title if you have a name for your quilt.

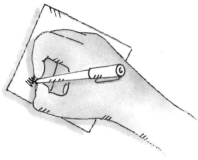

Stitch the label to the back of the quilt using a blanket stitch (see page 11). Start and stop with a loop knot (see page 9).

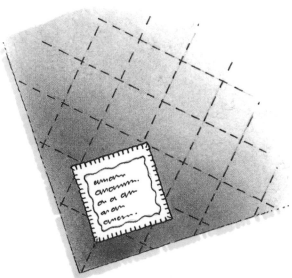